Math Monsters

KEEPING TRACK OF TIME
Go Fly a Kite!

Based on the Math Monsters™ public television series, developed in cooperation with the National Council of Teachers of Mathematics (NCTM).

by John Burstein

Reading consultant: Susan Nations, M.Ed., author/literacy coach/consultant

Math curriculum consultants: Marti Wolfe, M.Ed., teacher/presenter; Kristi Hardi-Gilson, B.A., teacher/presenter

WEEKLY WR READER®
EARLY LEARNING LIBRARY

Please visit our web site at: **www.earlyliteracy.cc**
For a free color catalog describing Weekly Reader® Early Learning Library's list
of high-quality books, call 1-877-445-5824 (USA) or 1-800-387-3178 (Canada).
Weekly Reader® Early Learning Library's fax: (414) 336-0164.

Library of Congress Cataloging-in-Publication Data

Burstein, John.
    Keeping track of time: go fly a kite! / by John Burstein.
       p. cm. — (Math monsters)
    Summary: The four monsters learn how to measure time when they share a kite
one windy day and want to take turns of the same length.
    ISBN 0-8368-3810-6 (lib. bdg.)
    ISBN 0-8368-3825-4 (softcover)
    1. Time measurements—Juvenile literature. [1. Time measurements.] I. Title.
  QB209.5.B875   2003
  529'.7—dc21
                            2003045048

This edition first published in 2004 by
Weekly Reader® Early Learning Library
330 West Olive Street, Suite 100
Milwaukee, WI 53212 USA

Text and artwork copyright © 2004 by Slim Goodbody Corp. (www.slimgoodbody.com).
This edition copyright © 2004 by Weekly Reader® Early Learning Library.

Original Math Monsters™ animation: Destiny Images
Art direction, cover design, and page layout: Tammy Gruenewald
Editor: JoAnn Early Macken

Printed in the United States of America

1 2 3 4 5 6 7 8 9 07 06 05 04 03

You can enrich children's mathematical experience by working with
them as they think about the Corner Questions in this book. Create
a special notebook for recording their mathematical ideas.

Time and Math

Time is a difficult concept for young children to grasp. Exploring the
passage of time by using a variety of measurement tools helps
expand children's understanding of this abstract concept.

Meet the Math Monsters™

ADDISON

Addison thinks
math is fun.
"I solve problems
one by one."

Mina flies
from here to there.
"I look for answers
everywhere."

MINA

MULTIPLEX

Multiplex
sure loves to laugh.
"Both my heads
have fun with math."

Split is friendly
as can be.
"If you need help,
then count on me."

SPLIT

We're glad you want to take a look
at the story in our book.

We know that as you read, you'll see
just how helpful math can be.

Let's get started. Jump right in!
Turn the page, and let's begin!

One sunny day, Mina said to the other
Math Monsters,
   "Let's go out and fly our kite
   way up in the sky.
   It will be a pretty sight
   flying up so high."

"I will fly it first," said Multiplex.
"No, I will," said Mina.
"I want to fly it," said Split.

When you and a friend both want to play with the same toy, what do you do?

"Let's take turns and share," said Addison. "That way, we all can fly the kite."

All the monsters agreed.

Multiplex went first. He flew the kite for a long, long time.

"May I go now?" asked Addison.

"Sure," said Multiplex. He handed the kite string to Addison.

How do you feel when a friend shares with you?

7

"Thank you for sharing," said Addison. "I love flying a kite."

As soon as Addison began
to fly the kite, Split said, "My turn.
Your time is up."

"I just started," said Addison.

*If Addison gets
a shorter turn
than Multiplex,
is that fair?*

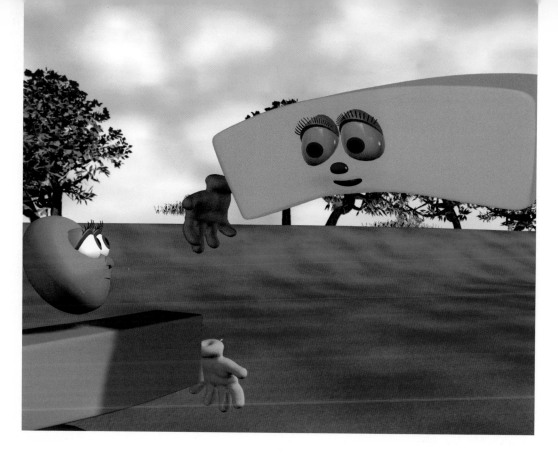

"That is not fair," said Mina. "Multiplex flew the kite for a much longer time than Addison. To be fair, all of us need to fly the kite for the same time."

"What can we do?" asked Split.

The monsters came up with a plan
to keep track of time by counting.

"Multiplex can fly the kite until
I count to ten," said Addison.

"Addison can fly the kite until
I count to ten," said Split.

"Split can fly the kite until I count
to ten," said Mina.

"Mina can fly the kite until
I count to ten," said Multiplex.

*Do you think this
plan is fair?*

11

"That sounds fair," said Mina.

Multiplex sent the kite high up into the air.

Addison counted very, very slowly. "1 . . . 2 . . . 3 . . . 4 . . . 5 . . . 6 . . . 7 . . . 8 . . . 9 . . . 10. My turn," he said.

Addison took the string. He began to fly the kite.

Split counted very fast. "1, 2, 3, 4, 5, 6, 7, 8, 9, 10! My turn," she said.

If Split counts faster than Addison, is that fair?

"That is not fair," said Mina. "Multiplex had more time to fly the kite."

"We both counted to ten," said Split.

"Yes, but you counted much faster. Addison had a much shorter turn," said Mina.

It was getting hot out. Addison went to get a drink of water.

"Let's take some time to think," he said.

Do you ever take time to think about a problem? Is it helpful?

Addison lifted his cup to take a drink.

He saw something.

"Oh no," he said. "There is a hole in my cup.

The water is drip, drip, dripping out."

"That gives me an idea," said Split. "We can use the drips to keep track of our time flying the kite."

How do you think the drips can help keep track of time?

"The drips from the cup drip at the same speed,"
said Split. "Ten drips for Multiplex will take the same
time as ten drips for Addison."

"We can each fly the kite for ten drips. We will all
have the same kite-flying time," said Mina.

"Ten drips is too short," said Multiplex. "Let's count
twenty drips."

Multiplex flew the kite for twenty drips.

His monster friends watched and counted.

How many drips should Addison get?

Addison flew the kite for twenty drips.

"This is fun and fair," he said.

Then Mina flew the kite for twenty drips. So did Split.

How do you
think Split's
plan worked?

"This really works!" said Multiplex. "Everybody had the same number of drips. We all got to fly for the same time."

"Let's go again," said Mina.

The wind grew much stronger.

Multiplex took his next turn. The kite lifted him. It took him up, up, up for a ride.

"You are not flying the kite," said Mina. "The kite is flying you!"

Multiplex came back down. The monsters took turns flying through the sky. They sang,

"We each have time, time to fly
this pretty kite into the sky.
It is such fun to be so high
looking down and sailing by."

What are some other ways people measure time?

ACTIVITIES

Pages 5, 7 Talk with children about ways they can share and take turns when playing with friends or siblings. This is a great opportunity to role-play kindness with playmates.

Pages 9, 11 Discuss the meaning of the word "fair" in the context of the story. What the monsters are really trying to establish is an equal amount of time for each of them to fly the kite.

Page 13 Let children try counting to ten at different rates of speed — slowly at first and then very quickly. Help them understand why counting to ten is not a reliable way to measure the passage of time.

Page 15 Explain to children that sometimes when facing a difficult problem, it helps to take a break and think things through. That might help them see things in a new way.

Pages 17, 19, 21 Help children make their own cup timer. Using a paper clip, poke a small hole in the bottom of a plastic foam cup. Fill it with water and observe. Use this cup to explore the problems and model the monsters' solutions. Have fun with measuring and comparing the time it takes to do everyday activities such as brushing teeth, tying shoes, and putting away blocks.

Page 23 Talk about all the kinds of clocks and timers there are and how they are used around your home and in the world. For example, they help you get up in the morning, they help you bake a cake, they help determine the winner of a race. Have fun thinking of other ways to use these timing tools.